BEMOE

Dwight Baltimore

ISBN: 978-1-967375-02-8 (Paperback)

ISBN: 978-1-963565-19-5 (Ebook)

Library of Congress Control Number: 2024913583

Printed in the United States of America

Published by

info@thequippyquill.com

(302) 295-2278

Table of Contents

Acknowledgments

My Wife and Daughter
Sister and Brother
Descendants of Della Harrison
The Ewing Family
The Tolbert Family
George and Agnes Augustus Family
John and Mamie Banks Family
Dwight Morrow High School Class of 1996
Dr. James Still Education Center
Westover 5
H. Reed, A.B. Best, R. Watson, K Davis & I
Redline Motor Touring Club
Divas for a Cure
Nate, Herb
Brother Wolf Young Blood
Original Eight Chapters of the National Association
and Trooper Motor Cycle Club

At 11:05 A.M., JUNE 28, 1947, in Old Riverside Hospital across town Newport News, Virginia, I made my entrance to this world. I was born to Naomi Harrison and DeWitt Cooke. My mother was in labor for eighteen hours, waiting for the doctor who was somewhere fishing. My first ride was in a Cadillac. It was the funeral director's hearse.

Since I was eight or nine years old, I have been in love with and have always wanted to own a motorcycle. In the next few pages, I would like to tell you how the love started and some adventures I have experienced over the years.

I spent my summers in Newport News, Virginia in Old Newsome Park 1079 48th street. I spent the summers with my Uncle George and my Aunt Agnes, my mother's sister. Next door, lived a lady named Ms. Sarah and her four children. James Earl, was the oldest son, who had a 1951 '52 Harley Davidson motorcycle. I remembered the name Harley Davidson on the tank and the large seat with the big springs. The Harley was parked outside the backdoor of Ms. Sarah's house. James Earl was in the Military at the time, and the bike just sat there day in and day out.

I would spend a lot of my summer days sitting on the big old seat bouncing up and down, holding on to the wide handlebars, and pretending I was on a road trip to anywhere from Virginia to New Jersey. I fell in love with that motorcycle. I remember saying, "When I grow up, I was going to buy myself a motorcycle."

My cousin Glenn and I would build and modify bicycles with small wheels in the front and stock wheel in the rear. We would get old chrome chair legs, flatten one end, drill holes in them, and mount them to the rear axle to make artificial exhaust pipes to make our bike look like a motorcycle. We would put a baseball card using clothespins on the front and rear spokes to make a noise like an engine.

I can remember one summer, my father was sitting on the front porch telling me, "Bemoe, don't ride your bicycle in the street."

It wasn't five minutes before I caused a car to jam on its brakes. I had to be on the street if I was supposed to be riding on a motorcycle!

In high school, I worked after school at Nate Thomas Auto Body Shop. This was where I rode my first motorbike. It was the boss's motorbike bought from Sears and Roebuck. To show how bright I was, I rode it in the snow. I did not only do it once but also several times. It was not until I had to stop that I had problems. The slide seemed as if I was never going to stop. There were several times I had to find something to help me stop. Good thing there was no traffic. As the saying goes, "The Lord looks out for babies and fools." That's me!

When I went into the Air Force stationed in the Philippines, I was amazed at how the motorcycles were used for taxis. They were mopeds and small cc motorbikes.

KZ 900 KAW

SEVERAL YEARS AFTER GETTING OUT of the Air Force, I bought my first motorcycle. It was a 1976 blue-on-blue, KZ900, Kawasaki. Talking about a powerful machine, especially for someone who never rode a large-engine motorcycle before, I had to have a coworker ride it home.

While trying to learn how to ride this monster, I fouled the plugs, driving it too slow up and down the block.

Pete, a friend of mine and coworker, told me I had to take the motorcycle out and run it. I got my courage up and took the machine out.

How sensitive was the throttle, and how much power this machine had?

I found out on the back streets of Englewood, New Jersey, it was Green Street off of Englewood Avenue. I pulled the first wheelie. You best believe not by choice. I was in first gear, just getting ready to go into second gear when a German shepherd came at me. I tightened my grip on the throttle and twisted without thinking. Again, I had no idea how much power this machine had. The front wheel came off the ground, and my ass tightened up. I remembered what the man in the store repeated several times, *"Hit the kill switch."* A very good lesson learned.

The motorcycle came down to a stop. I was on one side of the motorcycle and the dog on the other. I heard someone say, "He won't bite."

I looked up, and the owner was laughing his ass off. In between laughs, he gave a whistle, and the dog returned to where he came from. I did not see any humor in this situation at all.

I was doing pretty well learning how to ride after that. I hooked up with some guys in town. They were riding big bikes, 750 cc. They took me out for my first interstate ride. Route 80 W was fairly new, and the roads were very smooth. The lead guy had the throttle wide open. I had no windshield, and I was too scared to take my eyes off the road to look at the speedometer to see how fast we were going. I was scared, but it was a good scare. I loved the speed, the wind in my face, and the power between my legs. I knew then that I was hooked.

The guys taught me how to back my bike in when we parked. I thought it was the coolest thing when I backed my Kaw in with a row of bikes. Things went well that summer. My girlfriend Roxie, now my wife, took Saturday and Sunday rides. The trips that stuck in my mind were the trips to Bear Mountain, New York, and Delaware Water Gap. I think that of all my motorcycles, the Kawasaki was the one Roxie liked the best.

One day while out riding by myself, I learned a good lesson: never pass a car on the right side. I T-boned the right passenger side of a VW Beetle, which was making a right turn into a driveway. The VW belonged to my cousin. That was the only good thing about the accident.

The bike went one way into the VW, and I went into a tuck and rolled to the right side of the motorcycle. I learned to always wear a helmet. From that day to this, I'm pro-helmet.

The cost of repair on the Kawasaki was too much for me to handle. I sold my Kaw to a guy in New York. I found later that he converted my bike into a race bike and was making big money.

I spent the rest of that summer and the summer of '78 and '79 without a motorcycle. After I sold my Kawasaki, it seemed like every time I would see a bike or a group of bikes on the road, my blood would start to boil. I knew deep inside I had to have another bike.

CB750F HONDA

Winter 1980

I WENT OUT JUST TO look and see what they had in the showroom; I came home with a 1979 CB750F Honda. It was 1500cc smaller than the Kaw, but I put 38,000 good road trip miles on it.

In 1982, I rode my first long-distance trip. I went to Nova Scotia with a friend CW who was riding a 550cc Honda.

CW and I did the trip in four days. The trip until today is still a blur. We left Willingboro, New Jersey, around 3:30 p.m. We ran into traffic in New York going across the George Washington Bridge and to Connecticut, we had a breakdown. We rode straight through the night to Bar, Harbor Maine.

The Ferry to Nova Scotia pulled out at 8:00 or 9:00 a.m. from Bar Harbor. We arrived about two hours before the boat launched. I was so tired I don't remember the boat ride to Nova Scotia.

Once in Nova Scotia, we rode from Yarmouth to Dartmouth. The roads were like glass, and there was only one traffic light that I can remember.

We were going to go through a national park until we saw a sign that read, Watch out for the Bears. We made a U-turn and headed back to Yarmouth. It seemed like we rode around the block, and we were back on the boat.

I had the biggest lobster I had ever seen on my plate. It was too big for the plate. I think the dinner cost $11.99 or so.

The ride back home was the same as going there – nonstop. We stopped only for gas. This trip stood out in my mind because it rained from the time we got off the boat in Maine until we got back to Willingboro, New Jersey. I must have poured six ounces of water from each boot. I learned another lesson. Buy a good rain suit.

Frederick, Maryland

CW AND I RAN ACROSS a flyer about a swap meet in Frederick. We decide to get up early and make the run. We figured it would take approximately two hours. We pulled out around 8:00 a.m. We reached our destination at about 10:00 a.m. The swap meet was located way back in the woods. We were one of the first to arrive.

We parked our Hondas in the rear of the parking lot next to the beer truck. For $3, we can buy a large cup and can drink all the beer we want. We thought this was going to be a pretty good trip. As the day went on, we found out that this was a Harley Davidson Swap Meet. CW and I had the only Hondas in the parking lot – the rear of the parking lot. Did I mention we were the only black guys out of six at this meet?

We decided to move our bikes toward the entrance. We made sure the state trooper saw us as we pushed our Hondas gently to the front of the parking lot, making sure we did not get too close or touch anyone's bike, and attempted to get as close to the trooper as possible.

At this point, we were not sure if we could trust the trooper. Remember that we were in the backwoods of Frederick, Maryland, with a bunch of redneck Harley riders drinking as much beer as they can hold. The Confederate flags were flying, and there were a lot of woods and trees. That tightening of ass returned.

We have our Hondas parked close to the entrance of the swap meet in the eye view of the trooper. We tried to fit in as well as possible, and things were going pretty well. The show bikes were lined up.

The vendors had their goods laid out, and more people were started to arrive.

While taking in the show, drinking our beer, looking over all the Harleys and stuff to buy for Harley, in a distance, a low roar could be heard. It was the sound of a pack of straight pipe Harley. The closer they got, the louder the roar. To be honest, it was a beautiful sound if you are into motorcycles.

We watched for the pack to arrive. They showed up. It must have been twenty to thirty bikes pulled up to the entrance. I'd been told they are called dirty neckers. On the lead bike was a redneck who must have weighed at least 375 pounds. And believe me, he was 100 percent redneck. I knew he was all redneck because he had a tee shirt on, that read, *'Looking for One Skinny Nigger to use for my Drive Belt for My Harley.'*

When CW saw that, he said to me, "I can get at least six of them." What? CW never left home without his pistol.

I said to CW, "There are a thousand of these motherfuckers out here. It's time to get our black asses out of here."

We slowly mounted our Hondas making sure the state trooper had an eyeball on us. We said goodbye to Frederick, Maryland. Lesson learned? Make sure you know where you're going and if you're invited.

Montreal, Canada

THE TRIP STARTED IN WILLINGBORO and was supposed to go to Montreal, Toronto, and back to Willingboro.

When you ride with two or more riders, you learn a lot about people and their attitudes. On this trip, I was riding with CW who upgraded to a 1984 1100cc, Honda Goldwing, which was purchased just before we made this trip. Cowboy's 1975 1000cc Honda was having fuel cock problems. Hurricane had a 1989 1100cc Honda Ninja and just wanted to ride. I had my 1979 750cc CB750F Honda.

Getting to Montreal, we had problems with Cowboy's fuel system and, having to stop every one hundred miles for gas. CW and Hurricane were getting annoyed with the stops. Remember they had newer machines; they wanted to ride. They could get 150 miles to a tank of gas.

I don't know if it was before the border or after that we had to tow Cowboy's machine. Being a new rider in long-distance riding before leaving on a trip, I would go over a list hanging in my garage, which reads, "Don't leave home without it."

On this list, one of the items was a rope. Being a smart biker, I had everything on the list packed on my bike. You will never know what is going to happen on the road. After towing Cowboy to a gas station and getting him running, we made it to Montreal and had a grand time that night.

The next morning while Cowboy was making repairs to his bike, CW decided that Cowboy's bike was not up to par to ride with, and he did not want to continue the trip. Cowboy and Hurricane went on to Toronto. Me, I couldn't see CW riding back home by himself, so I agreed to ride back home.

I learned, no more Mr. Nice Guy. This was one of the trips I kept saying to myself, I wish I went to the whole trip. Besides the bike problems, attitudes, and Montreal drivers, the trip was one to be remembered.

Front Royal, Virginia

Front Royal, Virginia, Skyline Drive, Blue Ridge Mountain

ANOTHER FAST TRIP.

I was riding with a 1975 1000cc Honda Goldwing, owned by Cowboy, and a 1981 1100cc, Honda Hurricane, owned by Hurricane Sam.

I had a new experience – hairpin turns. Do you remember I was telling you about ass-tightening up before when the dog came at me? Hairpin turns can make things tighten up as well. Skyline Drive on Blue Ridge Mountain was very beautiful. I would suggest every biker make this run. I would like to do it again, taking my time to enjoy all of Skyline Drive.

We started at Front Royal, Virginia, the start of the Skyline Drive. We rode to Route 64. Once off the mountain and on Route 64, we stopped for lunch.

Cowboy showed Sam and me his right boot. Cowboy had dragged his right boot in all the right turns coming down the mountain. Cowboy put a hole in his boot. You could see his socks, and that is not a fish story.

While having lunch, I explained to Cowboy and Hurricane how we had to watch our speed and look out for the police on Route 64 East. We were headed for Newport News, Virginia.

Cowboy took the lead. We were going about 70 mph. All of a sudden, a Cadillac passed us doing at least 90 mph. With this, Cowboy picked up speed. While trying to catch the Caddy, we passed a black Chevy SS.

I thought I saw a patch on his left shoulder. I thought it was a security guard. We were going too fast to get a good look. About a mile down the road, I saw these blue lights flashing from the grill of the Chevy SS in my rearview mirror. I heard, "Pull over and no funny stuff," coming from a loudspeaker.

The police officer got out of his car and asked, "Do you know how fast you were going?" No one replied. The officer said, "If I tell you how fast you were going, I will have to lock you up."

One by one, the police officer invited us to his car and gave us each speeding ticket. We could not say too much. It was either the ticket or go to jail.

When it was my turn in the car, I asked about the Caddy that passed us. The officer said he never saw it. The rest of the trip into Newport News was within the speed limit.

Lake George, New York

My first trip to Lake George, New York, Americade 1989

AMERICADE IS ONE OF THE largest organized bike rallies on the East Coast, which happens during the first week of June.

Cowboy was on his 1975 1000cc Honda Goldwing and I was on my 1979 750cc CB750F Honda. This more than three-hundred-mile trip seemed to never end. Not knowing where we were going, we made reservations late, and the only accommodation we could find was on a horse farm. The entrance was uphill. This was no problem until it started to rain. We had to go up and down mud and horse-shit trail to and from our cabin. I learned another new experience – motorcycles, mud, horse shit, and rain do not mix.

Americade made up for the conditions coming and going to town. The town of Lake George was taken over by motorcycles. Both sides of the street were filled with bikes. There were all kinds of bikes and all kinds of people on Canada Street in Lake George, New York.

The roads in upstate New York were great. You've got the mountains and curves, covered bridges and beautiful farmland and old towns, the Ausable Chasm. If you don't want to ride, staying in the town of Lake George can be just great.

The bikes started to arrive in Lake George early on Wednesday, and by Friday, the sounds of motorcycles were heard coming from miles.

On Saturday, a parade was formed at a staging area by the lake. You ride into town heading north on Canada Street, and you do a U-turn at the end of town, and then you head back south on Canada Street onto Cadillac Mountain to end with a barbecue.

Being our first trip to Americade, we had to ride in the parade. Like all parades, the speed was slow. The CB750F, not being water cooled engine started to overheat and started fouling out. But I made it.

I had made ten trips to Americade. I had been in one and only one parade. With no exaggeration, there must have been 300 to 500 bikes in the parade. In the staging area, we lined up forming the word *Americade*. A picture was taken by helicopter. If you can find a 1989 Americade magazine, you can see me in the parade formation. You might need a microscope to see Cowboy and I, but we will in there.

Friday night in Lake George, the parade on Saturday, and the Tour Expo – this was the largest motorcycle shopping expo in the area. If you can't find it at a Tour Expo, you won't find it. This is what Americade is all about – the meeting of new and old friends. Did I mention all the motorcycles?

Even though it rained for four days, the trip was one of my best. All the trips to Lake George had been great. I guess that was why I had been to Americade ten times, and I plan to go again.

Solo

EVERY YEAR, RETURNING FROM LAKE GEORGE, I would share my story with guys and girls about Americade. Every year, I had people tell me that they were going to ride to Lake George the following June.

I start planning for my trip three months in advance. I get the maps out, I think of what clothes I'm going to take, figure out how I'm going to pack the bike, what is going to go where on the bike, and last but not least, going over the bike to make sure it is ready to roll.

Leading up to the day of departure, I was supposed to have five guys ride to Lake George with me. On the day of departure, everyone backed out. I got all kinds of, "It's going to rain" or "My wife and I were talking," etc.

So be it. I pulled out at the scheduled time, 6:30 a.m. Questions were going on inside my head. Suppose I break down was the biggest. Again, so be it.

Getting on the New Jersey turnpike, there was a chill in the air. No, it was cold. I asked myself, *Should I pull over and add some more clothing?* I told myself to ride a little bit further. With the sun rising to my right, it was a beautiful sight. I was riding north watching the big red-orange-yellow ball get larger and larger while rolling along at around 70 mph, passing the Newark Airport, and watching the planes land and take off. The air was not the best to breathe, but I was only in the area for a short time.

Before I knew it, I was paying my toll at the end of the turnpike. I'd only been riding for one hour and twenty minutes.

I got off the turnpike and onto the Palisades Interstate Parkway. I was still cold, but I thought as the day went on. *It will get warmer*. I felt my bladder getting tight. I knew there was not a rest area for miles.

It was approximately 8:00 a.m. No one will be on the lookout. I will make a short pit stop. Looking over the Hudson River into New York, I killed two birds with one stone. I took care of business and took a few minutes to watch a ship come down the river. Riding by myself was becoming all right. No one was saying let's go or wait for someone.

My next stop was the first rest area of Route 87 in New York State. I needed something warm in my system. I got a large cup of coffee. I held the cup for a while just to warm my hands. A few other bikers were in the same place, all saying the same thing. "It's cold out!"

Everyone was headed to the same place. I was invited to ride along in with the group, but I declined. I liked being by myself. Ten to fifteen minutes later, I was on the road. There was a talk about a trooper fifteen or twenty miles off the side up the highway with radar. I think I passed him doing 80 mph.

I'm headed for Albany on Interstate 87. The deep, rich green valleys and hills and miles of farmland made it seem like everything was clean and oh-so colorful. Some scenery looked like a picture. All you needed was a frame. As you passed the traffic and the traffic passed you, people would wave and complement the bike.

The children were the best. They look at you as if you were a superstar or an action figure. They would wave, and I would wave back or give a thumbs-up. They would give a big grin with bright eyes turning, telling their parents I waved at them. Then we get the smart-ass kids giving you the finger and pickling their noses.

The closer to Albany, the more motorcycles appeared. It was getting to the point where you really could not ride by yourself. I found myself riding at the tail of a pack because they were going too fast for me to pass them.

At the tollbooth in Albany, you had bikes on the side of the road before and after the tollbooth. Passing slowly, I would get a wave or a nod. I was scanning the bikes, looking to see if I knew anyone.

I was starting to get tired. I told myself I only had about an hour more of riding. It wounded up being more like two hours and a half before I got off the machine. The seat was starting to get teeth, and it was starting to bite my ass.

When I got to the town of Lake George and I saw all the bikes lined up on both sides of the street, I forgot about my sore ass and fatigue. I got a second wind. I watched everyone watching me. I felt like I conquered the world, and I was on my victory lap.

1983 Aspencade Honda

AFTER TEN YEARS AND APPROXIMATELY 38,000 miles, I decided to take the Motorcycle Experienced Rider Safety Course in April 1992 at Glassboro State College. The best course I'd ever taken. I thought I could ride. I learned more in three days than what I thought I knew from fifteen years of riding. If you are a rider or plan on riding, please take this course.

April 26, 1992 – I successfully completed the experienced rider skill training course that met the requirements of the Motorcycle Safety Foundation.

The CB750F served me well besides burning my daughter on the exhaust pipe, leaving a scar the size of fifty cents apiece. The only problem I had was I needed more power between my legs. I needed some music. I was having a lot of problems with the chain. I have replaced the chain three times since I owned the machine.

Someone told me about a dealership in Somers Point, New Jersey, who was supposed to have good used bikes. I decided to take a ride and check it out. Mad Max and his 1981 1300cc Kawasaki took the ride with me.

When we arrived and looked around, we saw nothing that caught my eye. I explained what I was looking for and how much money I had. He told me he had something in the back that just came in. He explained from what he could see, that all it needed was cleaning. We went into the back of the shop in a shed. There it was, a 1983 1100cc Burgundy with a lot of chrome Aspencade Honda. It had 26,000 miles on it, and the price was right.

Mad Max informed me if I did not buy it, he would. I gave a deposit and told the salesman to service it and to call me when it was ready.

I sold the CB750F that same week and used that money to purchase the Aspencade.

Two weeks later, I brought it home.

The word was out that I got another bike. The boys were helping me tear it down, cleaning it up, and making it ready for the road. Just because the dealer serviced it, I had to put my personal touch on it. I couldn't wait to ride to Lake George.

Man, this machine has so much chrome on it. The pinstriping was perfect. It even had a trailer hitch. The rear lighted up like a Christmas tree. It had AM and FM stereo, CB radio. Talking about happy, I was as happy as a monkey playing with a football.

My trip to Lake George on my new machine was like upgrading from a Chevrolet to a Cadillac. I think I used a whole can of wax on the new machine. I used the old "rub-on, rub-off" method. The chrome shined so bright it could hurt your eyes from the sun's reflection.

While riding around, I ran into another Harley swap met. Several girls were waving in bikes claiming they were getting ready to have a contest. I really did not have anything to do, so I went in and entered my bike in the foreign full-dresser classification. I won first place. I received a biker wallet with a chain. I think the rest of that trip was cleaning and admiring my new toy.

I put approximately 26,000 miles on this bike. Lake George added lots of miles to the bike.

Rallies

National Roundup

BLACK MOTORCYCLE CLUBS IN THE USA organized the rally. The clubs meet every year the first week in August. The rally is held someplace different every year. I attended my first roundup in 1994 in Atlanta, Georgia, and Greenville, South Carolina, in 1999. I planned on attending the roundup in Dinwiddie, Virginia, in 2002.

Black Bike Week, Memorial Day Weekend, Atlantic Beach, Myrtle Beach, South Carolina, 1997

This was a very interesting trip. This was where the party was. How would I rate it? Wild. This rally was for young folks and crotch rockets. I just want to see the video when you return.

Troubleman, riding a 1987 1200cc Royal Yamaha and I, towed our bikes to South Carolina. Troubleman informed me he had family and friends in Florence, South Carolina, and wanted to take a trip to visit. The trip sounded good to me.

It was just too much motorcycle congestion in Myrtle Beach anyway. The distance to Atlantic Beach from Myrtle Beach was approximately fifteen miles. The party was in Atlantic Beach. Our hotel was in Myrtle Beach. It took thirty to forty minutes to get from one end to the other.

The following morning, we pulled out early afternoon. We got onto Route 501 to Florence, South Carolina. It took us twenty minutes to get out of Myrtle Beach. Route 501 was a two-lane road with no shoulder. On both sides of the road, there were only woods and trees with paths wide enough for cars or small trucks going into the woods. Route 501 had just been paved and had a 55 mph speed limit. I never saw the speed limit posted.

Thirty miles outside of Myrtle Beach, Troubleman and I were riding a little more than the double nickels. I looked in my rearview mirror, and I saw a Mustang behind me with a flashing light. The officer said, "Pull off the highway."

I pulled as close to the grass to keep from going in the grass and having the bike slide. He said, "I said, off the highway." I pushed the bike into the grass. By this time, he had pulled up beside me in the grass.

Troubleman was parked about thirty yards in front, watching the cop talk to me.

The officer looked up at me and said, "When the police in New Jersey tell you, boys, to pull over, don't you pull over."

I replied, "Yes, sir."

The officer replied, "Do you know what the speed limit was?"

I told him, "I did not see it posted."

The officer replied, "Damn, a dummy knows the speed limit is fifty nationwide." I agreed with him.

The officer asked, "Do you know what I do for a living?"

"Yes, sir, you're a police officer."

He said, "I give tickets. When I wake up in the morning, I ask myself, how many tickets am I going to give out today?"

At this point, I was ready to say, *Give me the damn ticket and let us go.*

The officer said, "If you boys are going to New Jersey, I wish you a safe trip. If you plan on going back to Myrtle Beach and I see you, I'm giving you a ticket. Have a nice day."

The officer then peeled out in front of me, spraying grass and dirt on me and my bike.

I pulled my bike up to Troubleman, and I repeated the conversation I had with the cop.

Troubleman asked, "Why didn't you tell him to kiss your ass?"

My reply to Trouble was, "Do you see all the trees around us? Do you see these paths going off into woods? Do you know we are still in South Carolina?"

Needless to say, we came back a different route.

Breakfast Run

April 1999

THE WEATHER WAS JUST RIGHT for the first Sunday breakfast run. First Sunday, a bunch of guys would meet at Cheltenham Avenue and Broad Street, Philadelphia, for a breakfast run. This first Sunday, we decided to stay on the Jersey side.

Troy rode a 1980 1100 Honda Goldwing; Sonny rode a 1990 1500 Honda Aspencade Honda; and Tony rode a 1987 1200 Royal Yamaha.

We rode Route 29 North to Flemington, New Jersey, and along the Delaware River. The morning was crisp, but the sun was shining, and the roads were dry. Traffic was light. A lot of bicycles were out riding. When we got to Flemington, we stopped for breakfast like we do on our normal first Sunday breakfast run. We talked about where we had been, people, and their motorcycles, and things that were coming up.

After breakfast, we headed back to Willingboro. Mind you, I had been in the lead since the start of the trip.

We got back on Route 295 South. The traffic was light; the sky was clear, bright blue. The sun was warming the earth. It had been a very good morning run.

When you pass Burlington, New Jersey, there is a sign that reads, "Willingboro 2 miles." As soon as I passed this sign, Troy flew past me, next was Tony, and Sonny stayed behind me. I couldn't have them pass me and not keep up or get away from me, so I increased my speed.

I was doing approximately 90 mph when I noticed a slight vibration in the front end. I let off the gas and drove toward the shoulder. The slower the bike, the worse the vibration got. When I got to the shoulder of the highway, the last thing I saw was sixty-six on the speedometer. The bike vibrated violently and threw me off the right side of the bike like a bucking bronco.

I remembered bouncing onto the pavement of the highway shoulder and then rolling in the grass. It seemed as if I was not ever going to stop rolling.

I was facedown when I did the stop rolling. I remembered saying, "Oh shit, oh shit, oh shit." I moved my fingers. They were okay. I moved my toes and legs, and they seemed okay.

I heard voices. "Are you okay? Don't move. I'm a doctor I'm going to check for broken bones."

He started at the back of my skull and worked down. When he got down by my waist, I asked him. "You are not gay, are you?"

He replied with laughter in his voice. He was okay.

When I rolled over and sat up, I was looking for my bike. Troy, Tony, and Sonny said I did not want to see the bike.

People were collecting items that came off the bike for me. Everyone was so helpful and cordial.

I went to the hospital They took X-rays of my legs. They could not find any broken bones and no cuts. All they found was the rear of my legs from my ass to my calf were badly bruised. I was blessed, and I gave thanks to the American Motorcycle Association, Motorcycle Safety Foundation, and most of all, God.

I was given a speeding ticket at the hospital. The officer said he would talk to the prosecutor. The prosecutor dropped the charges of speeding to riding an unsafe vehicle. The ticket cost $150 anyway. The only good thing was, I did not get any points on my license.

My motorcycle was totaled. It was only April, and the bike sat in the garage beyond repair. My thighs, from my butt to my ankles, were black and blue, and I was feeling the pain of being thrown off my Honda at 66 mph, thinking my riding days were over.

My so-called friends were taking parts of my prized possessions like buzzards.

I sold salvage parts, a new timing chain, two tires, and the bike for $300. I just wanted the bike out of my garage.

Talking about a sad summer. My so-called buddies stopped coming by. I was missing the first Sunday breakfast runs. Most of all, I was missing my machine.

I went to the roundup that August. I was like a fish out of water. Three thousand motorcycles and I did not have one. I saw a bike just like mine for sale. The owner had the title with him, and the price was right. I told myself, my riding days are over, and I let the deal pass me by.

Buzzard Luck

Spring 2000

SOME FRIENDS WHO WORK FOR Public Service Electric and Gas Co. informed me of a coworker who just bought a brand-new Heritage Softail Harley and wanted to sell his 1984 1200 Aspencade Honda. I gave the owner a call. I told him I just wanted to see the bike, and I was not really sure if I wanted to buy the bike.

The Honda was as clean as the new Harley was. The owner explained that he was having battery problems. Other than that, the bike was in great shape. The bike had 40,000 miles on it, and he wanted $1,300 for it. I could not let this one get away.

I bought the bike home. The wife was upset. I wondered if she was concerned about my well-being or the money I spent. I explained the deal I got. I don't think she heard a word I said.

The first thing I bought was a new battery, thinking the battery that was on the bike was just old. After taking a good day ride, I found out that the stator, which charges the battery, was bad.

In conversation with my mechanic and reading an article about the 1984 Aspencade in one of my motorcycle magazines, I found out that this was one of the problems that came with this year's Honda.

To change the stator, you have to pull the engine out. Now I see why I got the bike for such a good price.

My mechanic informed me that if we pull the engine, we might as well put a new clutch in. I had plans on taking my new machine to Lake George. The time was getting close to making plans for my trip. Troy, my mechanic, assured me that the job would be done in time.

We pulled the engine the Saturday before leaving for Lake George. We are thinking that we would remove and replace both the stator and clutch and mount the engine on the same day.

Murphy's Law! We had the wrong gaskets. Again, Troy assured me we would be going to Lake George that coming Wednesday.

Monday afternoon, the gaskets came in. Troy was not able to finish the job until Tuesday.

I was at the point where I was thinking of canceling the trip.

Tuesday night at approximately nine-thirty, the engine was back in. We started the bike to see if it would start up. We did not test the bike to see if the battery was charging.

We put my bike and Cowboy's bike on the trailer that night so that we would be ready to move out the following morning for New York.

Wednesday afternoon in Lake George, we pulled the bike off the trailer and started it up with no problems, except for an oil leak. This was corrected with a new oil filter and oil.

From Wednesday to Saturday, I put three hundred and fifty miles on the bike. The battery was charging, and the clutch worked fine. I was a happy camper. All the bike needed was a bath.

After a great four days, we loaded the bikes back on the trailer for our trip back home.

Sunday morning was a beautiful day. The sky was blue with no clouds. We pulled out around 7:00 a.m. We stopped for breakfast and talked about our past four days.

We were on Interstate 287 in New Jersey. I was driving. There was no traffic. The sun was shining with clear blue skies. I was driving about 65 mph.

Are you familiar with the new tall sound walls on the Interstate Highways? Well, up ahead about a hundred yards, I noticed a tree hanging over the sound wall. I figured it was just an old tree. When I got close to the tree, in my peripheral vision to the right, I saw the tree starting to fall. It was like a dream. The branches hit the windshield, and the trunk of the tree sheared the tops of both bikes. My bike caught most of the tree.

That's the kind of luck that I have. Cowboy's windshield and right mirror were damaged. Lucky for him, he had replacement parts. My front end, windshield, fairing, headlight, and mirrors were damaged to no repair.

We pulled over in disbelief. We waited for the police to fill out an accident report. The cop acted as if we caused the tree to fall.

Thinking once we get back home, we would call the insurance company, and they would take care of the damages for both bikes. The insurance company informed us that since no cars were involved with the accident, they were not liable.

The state of New Jersey said it was an act of nature, and they were not liable.

I estimated $1000 in damage for my bike, and no one will pay. It was early June, and I can't ride my motorcycle for the rest of the summer.

On the bright side, no one got hurt. The tree could have fallen in front or on top of the van, or we could have been riding the bikes, and the tree could have fallen in front of us.

Over the winter, I found another fairing, and JC Whitney had the other parts to restore my machine. With the help of my mechanic, Troy, and the guys at West Side Auto Body, the Honda was back together and looking good. I'd made several breakfast runs, and I was planning my trips for the summer of 2002. I was hoping my luck will change for the better. Murphy's Law! I just found out that I needed a water pump.

Buffalo Soldiers

WHEN I BECAME A NEW Jersey Buffalo Soldier, our former president, Brother Wolf, who was a past member of Redline Motor Touring Club. I was former president and one of the founders. Brother Wolf came to me and said, "Bemoe, I found the club for us."

He said, "These brothers ride."

The first time I saw the colors. The colors are the insignia of the club they belong to, the chapter they belong to, and the state, your club or your chapter is in. The colors really caught my eye. In Dinwiddie, Virginia, that's when I decided I was going to become a Buffalo Soldier.

Seeing the club insignias being worn by members of the National Association of Troopers Motorcycle Club from different states, I was hooked.

I believe it was J-Byrd at the Esquire's MC event in Mt. Holly, New Jersey.

The colors popped like that when I saw more than three soldiers together. I was invited to come to a meeting. I went to my first meeting at TC Costley's house, the founder of the New Jersey Chapter and the two-term National President of the National Association of Buffalo Soldiers and Troopers Motorcycle Club.

Buffalo Soldier Creed

I am a Buffalo Soldier, and as a Buffalo Soldier I will uphold the standards and traditions set forth by my Chapter and the National Association of Buffalo Soldiers and Troopers Motorcycle Club.

I am proud of my colors and the rich history they represent. I will wear my color with pride and will do all within my power to educate the general public about the rich history of the 9th and 10th Cavalry Buffalo Soldiers.

I will respect my colors and my Buffalo Soldier Sisters and Brothers, and when my riding days come to an end, I wish to be remembered as one who served with Dignity as a responsible biker and a proud Buffalo Soldier.

This was where I learned about 1866 and the Buffalo Soldier. I said to myself, "I don't remember learning about these great black men in school."

I felt like I was in over my head and felt intimidated not knowing my history and how they wanted to project a positive image when riding their motorcycles. My first ride was to North, Virginia with the Buffalo Soldiers.

We met at a gas station on Route 38 in Hainesport, New Jersey. Birdman, Doc Toes, Teddy Bear and I were probes and the first to show up. We had no idea what our day was going to be like.

Doc Toes and Teddy Bear would ride a hundred miles to meet up with us ride 100 miles and then ride back home. We were told by TC that the forecast predicted chances of rain. When we pulled out at 6:30 a.m., it was a little misty. By the time we got to the Delaware Memorial Bridge, it was pouring.

When we arrived in North, Virginia, it had just stopped raining but with heavy overcast. We had enough time to get hamburgers and get our backs beat out, hearing the buffalo soldier chant, and seeing brothers laughing and enjoying being buffalo soldiers. Presidents and Vice Presidents having a private conference and me wanting to know what they were talking about.

I noticed a very large black cloud coming overhead, and in the distance, we heard, "Okay, Jersey, mount up."

I said to myself, "Can't we wait until the storm blows over?" Back on my machine with bolts of lightning in the sky, we headed back north.

We did stop for shelter wet like that at a gas station. Again, why stop at a gas station with lightning bolts dancing in the black sky? We had just enough time to get gas and go. I do remember him coming to a meeting in the snow on his bike, another probe wanting to be in this newly founded club for true riders, and to teach about Buffalo Soldiers of 1866.

I can say in more than twelve years of being with the Buffalo soldiers, the rides might had been rough, but the events had all been great. To top it off, I attended the National Buffalo Soldiers and Troopers Motorcycle Club Convention in Hampton, Virginia. Right next to where I was born and fell in love with motorcycles, in Newport News Virginia.

What a way to retire and still be able to ride.

To my New Jersey mother chapter family, and all my sisters and brothers of the National Association Buffalo Soldiers Troopers Motorcycle Club, please ride safely!

AUTHOR'S MESSAGE

Dwight "Bemoe" Baltimore, is a United States Air Force veteran, has a wonderful message for you who is interested in motorcycles, or considering getting involved in the bike lifestyle.

"Looking back on life and being blessed in seeing my dreams as a young man come to light. For those who ride motorcycles—if you're thinking of riding or just want to read about the life of one whose dream came true in the motorcycle world," said Baltimore.